Jagdterrier Dog Breed

Things You Need to Know about The Fierce Little Hunter

Copyright © 2021

All rights reserved.

DEDICATION

The author and publisher have provided this e-book to you for your personal use only. You may not make this e-book publicly available in any way. Copyright infringement is against the law. If you believe the copy of this e-book you are reading infringes on the author's copyright, please notify the publisher at: https://us.macmillan.com/piracy

Jagdterrier Dog Breed

Contents

Introduction 1

History 4

Appearance 11

Temperament 16

Jagdterrier Health 23

Caring for A Jagdterrier 30

Feeding 41

Average Cost to Keep for Jagdterrier 45

How to Identify A Jagdterrier 48

Jagdterrier Dog Breed

Introduction

Jagdterriers are small dogs that originate from Germany where they were originally bred to work both above and below ground tracking their prey. They have always been highly prized for their hunting abilities in their native land and Europe in general where Jagdterriers are still used to hunt larger game like wild boar and smaller quarry like badgers, foxes and weasels.

Jagdterrier Dog Breed

Although lesser known here in the UK, the Jagdterrier is a smart looking little dog and one that's highly intelligent with the added bonus being they form strong bonds with their families and owners which in short means they are not only very good working dogs, but they make great companions and family pets too. With this said, the breed is not Kennel Club recognised and very few well-bred puppies are available every year which means that anyone wanting to share a home with a Jagdterrier would need to register their interest with breeders for the pleasure of doing so.

Positives

Jagdterriers are loyal, affectionate companions and family pets

They thrive on having something to do

They are low maintenance on the grooming front

They shed moderately throughout the year

They are highly intelligent and in the right hands, easy to train

They are good around children

Jagdterrier Dog Breed

They are known to be a healthy breed

They don't mind being on their own providing it's never for too long

They are good "watchdogs", but not very good "guard dogs"

Negatives

Jagdterriers have an extremely high prey drive

They are not a good choice for first time dog owners

They are better suited to people who lead active, outdoor lives

They cannot be trusted around smaller animals and pets

They are expert escape artists

They are known to like the sound of their own voices

History

Jagdterriers were developed to be hunting dogs in their native Germany where they have always been highly prized for their skills at tracking down small and larger prey. The goal of breeders and genetic enthusiasts alike, was to create the perfect German working terrier that would not only be rated as being as good as American and British breeds, but even better.

Terriers were hugely popular throughout Europe in the early 1900's. They were also immensely popular in the United States. The largest dog show in the world was to be established in the UK at the end of the World War I which was to become known as Crufts although at first it was called the Allied Terrier Show. At the time, there was also a publication that was founded dedicated to dogs and more especially to Fox Terriers.

It was a time when "show" dogs rather than working-types became hugely popular. As such many working qualities of terriers were lost and this included their scenting skills as well as their endurance, stamina, keenness and determination along with their acute hearing and keen vision. Many Fox Terrier breeders and enthusiasts were not keen on seeing so many changes in working terrier lines and set up what was to become known as the German Fox Terrier Association with the end goal being to retain the hunting abilities and traits of terriers.

Jagdterrier Dog Breed

At the end of the First World War, the members of the German Fox Terrier Association broke with the club to set up their own project which was to develop the "perfect" German terrier. One of the members, a man called Zangenberg was given or purchased black Fox Terrier puppies that were sire by an English Terrier. There were 2 females and 2 males in the litter which were all wire-haired puppies with black coats and red markings. These puppies were to become the foundation dogs for the Jagdterrier and their names were Werwolf, Raughgraf, Morla and Nigra von Zangenberg.

A man called Lutz Heck who was the curator at the Berlin Zoo and a keen hunter who also boasted an ardent interest in genetics joined the other members of the project to further their endeavours to develop the "perfect" terrier. Another man who helped develop the breed was Dr. Herbert Lackner and as many as 700 dogs were used in the breeding programme. No dogs were allowed to leave the kennels the whole time the breed was being developed and any terrier that did not meet their standards were disposed of.

Jagdterrier Dog Breed

It is thought that the foundation breeds used to create and develop the Jagdterrier could have been Fox Terriers, but it could have also been black and tan Fell Terriers and Welsh Terriers as well as Old English Terriers. In 1926, the German Hunting Terrier Club was established with the breed being first introduced onto the scene a year later in 1927. Jagdterriers were an immediate success not only with the German hunting fraternity but also with the military.

Jagdterrier Dog Breed

At the end of the Second World War, breed numbers had been decimated throughout Germany, but enthusiasts worked hard to save the Jagdterrier from disappearing off the face of the planet altogether. They outcrossed their remaining terriers with Lakeland Terriers, but this proved to be unsuccessful and the breeding programme was subsequently abandoned.

By the beginning of the 1950's, breed numbers however, began to rise without the need to outcross to other breeds. Over the years, the breed's popularity began to rise again in the native Germany as it did elsewhere in Europe because over time they earned themselves a reputation for being excellent working dogs and companions both in American where they are used as "tree dogs" to track down squirrels and raccoons. Although their numbers are still very low here in the UK, the Jagdterrier is gaining popularity although anyone wishing to share their home with one would need to register their interest with breeders because so few puppies are bred every year.

The breed is not recognised by The Kennel Club, but Jagdterriers are

Jagdterrier Dog Breed

recognised by other international organisations which includes the American Kennel Club and the UKC as well as a few other international breed clubs. As previously mentioned, Jagdterriers are seldom seen in the UK and anyone wanting to share a home with one would need to register their interest with breeders and go on a waiting list with the good news being the wait would be well worth it.

Interesting facts about the breed

Is the Jagdterrier a vulnerable breed? No, although they are quite rare in the UK and although they are gaining a big fanbase, anyone wanting to share a home with a Jagdterrier would need to register their interest with breeders and go on a waiting list for the pleasure of doing so

They are often called German Hunt Terriers in other parts of the world

Breed numbers fell dangerously low at the end of World War II

Jagdterriers are known to be one of the most tenacious terriers around

Traditionally, a Jagdterrier's tail was always docked, but since the law banning the procedure came into effect in 2007, tail docking is now illegal with the exception being for some working breeds and if a dog suffers from some sort of health issue that requires their tails to be docked. The procedure must be agreed and authorised before being performed by a qualified vet

Jagdterrier Dog Breed

Appearance

Height at the withers: Males 33 - 40 cm, Females 33 - 40 cm

Average weight: Males 9 - 10 kg, Females 7.5 - 8.5 kg

Jagdterriers are compact, sturdy little dogs that boast having an alert appearance. When working, they are athletic, energetic and quick off the mark, but when they are at rest they are regal looking although they always have a fiery expression in their eyes. Their heads are quite long being wedge-shaped with the area between a dog's ears being flat but tapering towards their eyes. They have a slight stop and shortish muzzles with nice prominent cheeks and extremely strong underjaws.

The Jagdterrier has a strong jaw with a perfect scissor bite where their upper teeth neatly overlap their lower ones and they have strong teeth. Their eyes are dark in colour and small being deeply set with dogs always having an alert, determined look about them. Their noses are black although dogs with more brown in their coats can have brown noses which is acceptable. Their ears are V-shaped and nicely in proportion to a dog's head being set quite high and carried forwards touching the side of the head.

Jagdterriers have strong, slightly arched, powerful necks that are a little broader at the shoulder than at the nape. Shoulders are sloping and long with dogs having well-muscled front legs that show a good amount of bone. They have deep chests that are not too broad and their ribs are well sprung and nicely laid back. Their bodies are sturdy and compact with dogs having short, level backs and well-muscled loins with flat croups.

Their hindquarters are well angulated and muscular showing a good amount of bone with dogs having long, sinewy and powerful back legs. Feet are oval shaped with a dog's front ones often being wider and larger than their back feet. Tails are well set which dogs carry gaily much like the Foxhound when they are working or alert.

When it comes to their coat, the Jagdterrier can either have a harsh or smooth coat as well as any kind of texture in between the two. However, their coats are thick and dense which offers terriers a lot of protection when working in rough undergrowth and in challenging conditions. The accepted breed colour under AKC rules is as follows:

Black with brown, red, yellow or lighter markings on eyebrows, chest,

Jagdterrier Dog Breed

legs and back-ends

Black and grey with brown, red, yellow or lighter markings on eyebrows, chest, legs and back-ends

Dark brown with brown, red, yellow or lighter markings on eyebrows, chest, legs and back-ends

Greyish black with brown, red, yellow or lighter markings on eyebrows, chest, legs and back-ends

Jagdterriers can have either a light or dark mask and a small amount of white both on their toes and chests is acceptable under the UKC's breed standard

Gait/movement

When a Jagdterrier moves, they do so with great purpose, speed and agility covering a log of ground when they do.

Faults

Jagdterrier Dog Breed

Prospective Jagdterrier owners should be wary of any puppies or dogs that show any sort of exaggeration whether in their looks or conformation and that extra-small dogs often come with many health issues so they are best avoided. A responsible breeder would always ensure that puppies they produce are of a good size and conformation and would avoid breeding extra small dogs for these reasons. Males should have both testicles fully descended into their scrotums.

Temperament

The Jagdterrier has always been highly prized for their intelligence and hunting abilities because they are such determined little dogs. In short, they are quick off the mark and will not give up until they achieve their goals all of which are traits that are deeply embedded in a dog's psyche even when they are in a home environment. They have a tremendous amount of stamina and energy which means they are best suited to people who live in a more rural environment and who lead active,

Jagdterrier Dog Breed

outdoor lives.

They are bold, courageous and always extremely alert, but very people oriented. They make good companions and family pets, but they are first and foremost working dogs. As such, they are not the best choice for first time owners, but a good choice for anyone who is familiar with the breed or this type of high energy working dog and who therefore understands and can satisfy their specific needs.

They have extremely high prey drives and are never happier than when they are outside doing what they have always been bred to do which is to track and hunt down their quarry both above and below ground. Puppies need to be well socialised from a young age and this must involve introducing them to lots of new situations, noises, people, other animals and dogs once they have been fully vaccinated so they mature into well-balanced, calm adult dogs.

Their training must start early paying particular attention to the "recall" command right from the word go and even then, if a Jagdterrier sees something in the distance they are likely to take off after it which is why care must be taken as to where and when they are allowed to run off their leads. They tend to be wary around people they don't know, but rarely would a Jagdterrier show any sort of aggressive behaviour towards a stranger, preferring to keep their distance until they get to know someone.

Are they a good choice for first time owners?

Jagdterriers are not a good choice for first time dog owners because they need to be socialised, handled and trained by people who are familiar with the specific needs of an intelligent, high-energy terrier with a low boredom threshold.

What about prey drive?

Having been bred to "work and hunt", a Jagdterrier has a very high prey drive and being so tenacious, they never give up. As such, great care must always be taken when they are around smaller animals and

Jagdterrier Dog Breed

pets. Care should also be taken as to where and when a Jagdterrier can run off the lead especially if there is wildlife or livestock close by, bearing in mind that if a terrier picks up a scent, they are likely to ignore the recall command and go off in search of what is at the end of it.

What about playfulness?

Jagdterriers have a very playful side to their natures. They are fun-loving and high-energy all rolled into one small package. They love to be entertained and to entertain which they do through their working abilities. They are known to be a little mischievous when the mood takes them and being so clever, a Jagdterrier quickly learns how to get their own way when they want something.

What about adaptability?

Jagdterriers may be small in stature, but they are high-energy characters that are better suited to living with people who lead active outdoor lives rather than being cooped up in an apartment. They were bred to work which is something that is deeply embedded in a terrier's psyche and if they are not put through their paces, they are very unhappy dogs.

What about separation anxiety?

Although Jagdterriers form strong ties with their families, they do not generally suffer from separation anxiety providing they are not left to their own devices for too long. If they do find themselves on their own for too long, a Jagdterrier would quickly find ways of amusing themselves, bearing in mind that they have a very low boredom threshold. This could see them being destructive around the home and barking incessantly to get someone's attention and to show how unhappy they are at the situation.

What about excessive barking?

A lot of Jagdterriers like the sound of their own voices a little too much which is something that needs to be gently nipped in the bud when a dog is still young being careful not to frighten them. Others will only bark when there are strangers about or when something they don't like is going on in their surroundings or when they have chased something to "ground".

Do Jagdterriers like water?

Most Jagdterriers love swimming and will take to the water whenever they can more especially when the weather is hot. However, if anyone who owns a dog that does not like water should never force them to go in because it would just end up scaring them. With this said, care should always be taken when walking a Jagdterrier off the lead anywhere near more dangerous watercourses just in case a dog decides to leap in and then needs rescuing because they cannot get out of the water on their own.

Are Jagdterriers good watchdogs?

Jagdterriers are natural watchdogs because they are always on the alert. With this said, rarely would a dog show any sort of aggressive behaviour preferring to keep their distance and bark as a way of alerting an owner to something they don't like that's going on.

Jagdterrier Health

Jagdterrier Dog Breed

The average life expectancy of a Jagdterrier is between 13 and 15 years when properly cared for and fed an appropriate good quality diet to suit their ages.

The Jagdterrier is known to be a robust, healthy dog and one that does not seem to suffer from the sort of hereditary and congenital health issues that plague many other breeds. This could be due to the fact there are so few dogs around and therefore not enough information has been gathered regarding their health. However, there have been reports of some dogs developing the following hereditary eye disorder:

Primary lens luxation (PLL) - dogs should be eye tested through the British Veterinary Association or the Animal Health Trust (AHT)

What about vaccinations?

Jagdterrier puppies would have been given their initial vaccinations before being sold, but it is up to their new owners to make sure they have their follow-up shots in a timely manner with the vaccination schedule for puppies being as follows:

10 -12 weeks old, bearing in mind that a puppy would not have full protection straight away, but would be fully protected 2 weeks after they have had their second vaccination

There has been a lot of discussion about the need for dogs to have boosters. As such, it's best to talk to a vet before making a final decision on whether a dog should continue to have annual vaccinations which are known as boosters.

What about spaying and neutering?

A lot of vets these days recommend waiting until dogs are slightly older before spaying and neutering them which means they are more mature before undergoing the procedures. As such they advise neutering males and spaying females when they are between the ages of 6 to 9 months old and sometimes even when a dog is 12 months old.

Other vets recommend spaying and neutering dogs when they are 6 months old, but never any earlier unless for medical reasons. With this said, many breeds are different and it is always advisable to discuss things with a vet and then follow their advice on when a dog should be spayed or neutered.

What about obesity problems?

Like other breeds, a Jagdterrier may gain weight after they have been spayed or neutered and it's important to keep an eye on a dog's waistline just in case they do. If a dog starts to put on weight it's important to adjust their daily calorie intake and to up the amount of exercise they are given. Older dogs too are more prone to gaining weight and again it's essential they be fed and exercised accordingly because obesity can shorten a dog's life by several years. The reason being that it puts a lot of extra strain on a dog's internal organs including the heart which could prove fatal.

What about allergies?

Some Jagdterriers are prone to suffering from allergies and it's important for a dog to see a vet sooner rather than later if one flares up. Allergies can be notoriously hard to clear up and finding the triggers can be challenging. With this said, a vet would be able to make a dog with an allergy more comfortable while they try to find out the triggers which could include the following:

Certain dog foods that contain high levels of grain and other cereal-type fillers

Airborne pollens

Dust mites

Jagdterrier Dog Breed

Environment

Flea and tick bites

Chemicals found in everyday household cleaning products

Participating in health schemes

All responsible Jagdterrier breeders would ensure that their stud dogs are tested for known hereditary and congenital health issues known to affect the breed by using the following scheme:

Testing for primary lens luxation (PLL) through the British Veterinary Association or the Animal Health Trust (AHT)

What about breed specific breeding restrictions?

There are no breed specific breeding restrictions in place for the Jagdterrier because they are not a Kennel Club recognised breed. With this said, all responsible breeders would follow the advice and recommendations as set out by the Kennel Club and Breed Association to ensure the continued good health and welfare of the breed.

Jagdterrier Dog Breed

What about Assured Breeder Requirements?

The Jagdterrier is not a recognised Kennel Club breed, as such there are no Assured Breeder requirements in place.

Caring for A Jagdterrier

As with any other breed, Jagdterriers need to be groomed on a regular basis to make sure their coats and skin are kept in top condition. They also need to be given regular daily exercise to ensure they remain fit and healthy. On top of this, dogs need to be fed good quality food that meets all their nutritional needs throughout their lives.

Caring for a Jagdterrier puppy

Jagdterrier puppies are boisterous and full of life which means it's essential for homes and gardens to be puppy-proofed well in advance of their arrival. A responsible breeder would have well socialised their puppies which always leads to more outgoing, confident and friendly dogs right from the word go. With this said, any puppy is going to feel vulnerable when they leave their mother and littermates which must be taken into account. The longer a puppy can remain with their mother, the better although it should never be for too long either.

It's best to pick a puppy up when people are going to be around for the first week or so which is the time needed for a puppy to settle in. Puppy-proofing the home and garden means putting away any tools and other implements that a boisterous puppy might injure themselves on. Electric wires and cables must be put out of their reach because puppies love chewing on things. Toxic plants should be removed from flowerbeds and the home too.

Jagdterrier Dog Breed

Puppies need to sleep a lot to grow and develop as they should which means setting up a quiet area that's not too out of the way means they can retreat to it when they want to nap and it's important not to disturb them when they are sleeping. It's also a good idea to keep "playtime" nice and calm inside the house and to have a more active "playtime" outside in the garden which means puppies quickly learn to be less boisterous when they are inside.

The documentation a breeder provides for a puppy must have all the details of their worming date and the product used as well as the information relating to their microchip. It is essential for puppies to be wormed again keeping to a schedule which is as follows:

Puppies should be wormed at 6 months old

They need to be wormed again when they are 8 months old

Puppies should be wormed when they are 10 months old

Jagdterrier Dog Breed

They need to be wormed when they are 12 months old

Things you'll need for your puppy

There are certain items that new owners need to already have in the

Jagdterrier Dog Breed

home prior to bringing a new puppy home. It's often a good idea to restrict how much space a puppy plays in more especially when you can't keep an eye on what they get up to bearing in mind that puppies are often quite boisterous which means investing in puppy gates or a large enough playpen that allows a puppy the room to express themselves while keeping them safe too. The items needed are therefore, as follows:

Good quality puppy or baby gates to fit on doors

A good well-made playpen that's large enough for a puppy to play in so they can really express themselves as puppies like to do

Lots of well-made toys which must include good quality chews suitable for puppies to gnaw on, bearing in mind that a puppy will start teething anything from when they are 3 to 8 months old

Good quality feed and water bowls which ideally should be ceramic rather than plastic or metal

A grooming glove

A slicker brush or soft bristle brush

Jagdterrier Dog Breed

Dog specific toothpaste and a toothbrush

Scissors with rounded ends

Nail clippers

Puppy shampoo and conditioner which must be specifically formulated for use on dogs

A well-made dog collar or harness

A couple of strong dog leads

A well-made dog bed that's not too small or too big

A well-made dog crate for use in the car and in the home, that's large enough for a puppy to move around in

Baby blankets to put in your puppy's crate and in their beds for when they want to nap or go to sleep at night

Keeping the noise down

All puppies are sensitive to noise including Jagdterrier puppies. It's important to keep the noise levels down when a new puppy arrives in the home. TVs and music should not be played too loud which could end up stressing a small puppy out.

Keeping vet appointments

As previously mentioned, Jagdterrier puppies would have been given their first vaccinations by the breeders, but they must have their follow up shots which is up to their new owners to organise. The vaccination schedule for puppies is as follows:

10 -12 weeks old, bearing in mind that a puppy would not have full protection straight away, but would only be fully protected 2 weeks after they have had their second vaccination

When it comes to boosters, it's best to discuss these with a vet because there is a lot of debate about whether a dog really needs them after a certain time. However, if a dog ever needed to go into kennels, their vaccinations would need to be fully up to date.

What about older Jagdterriers when they reach their senior years?

Jagdterrier Dog Breed

Older Jagdterriers need lots of special care because as they reach their golden years, they are more at risk of developing certain health concerns. Physically, a dog's muzzle may start to go grey, but there will be other noticeable changes too which includes the following:

Coats become coarser

A loss of muscle tone

Jagdterriers can either become overweight or underweight

They have reduced strength and stamina

Older dogs have difficulty regulating their body temperature

They often develop arthritis

Immune systems do not work as efficiently as they once did which means dogs are more susceptible to infections

Older dogs change mentally too which means their response time tends to be slower as such they develop the following:

They respond less to external stimuli due to impaired vision or hearing

They tend to be a little pickier about their food

They have a lower pain threshold

Become intolerant of any change

Often an older dog can feel disorientated

Living with a Jagdterrier in their golden years means taking on a few more responsibilities, but these are easily managed and should include taking a look at their diet, the amount of exercise they are given, how often their dog beds need changing and keeping an eye on the condition of their teeth.

Older Jagdterriers need to be fed a good quality diet that meets their needs at this stage of their lives all the while keeping a close eye on a dog's weight. A rough feeding guide for older dogs is as follows bearing in mind they should be fed highly digestible food that does not contain any additives:

Protein content should be anything from 14 – 21%

Fat content should be less than 10%

Fibre content should be less than 4%

Calcium content should be 0.5 – 0.8%

Phosphorous content should be 0.4 – 0.7%

Sodium content should be 0.2 – 0.4%

Older Jagdterriers don't need to be given the same amount of daily exercise as a younger dog, but they still need the right amount of physical activity to maintain muscle tone and to prevent a dog from putting on too much weight. All dogs need access to fresh clean water and this is especially true of older dogs when they reach their golden years because they are more at risk of developing kidney disorders.

Feeding

If you get a Jagdterrier puppy from a breeder, they would give you a feeding schedule and it's important to stick to the same routine, feeding the same puppy food to avoid any tummy upsets. You can change a puppy's diet, but this needs to be done very gradually always making sure they don't develop any digestive upsets and if they do, it's best to put them back on their original diet and to discuss things with the vet before attempting to change it again.

Older dogs are not known to be fussy eaters, but this does not mean they can be fed a lower quality diet. It's best to feed a mature dog twice a day, once in the morning and then again in the evening, making sure it's good quality food that meets all their nutritional requirements. It's also important that dogs be given the right amount of exercise so they burn off any excess calories or they might gain too much weight which can lead to all sorts of health issues. Obesity can shorten a dog's life by several years so it's important to keep an eye on their waistline from the word go.

Feeding guide for a Jagdterrier puppy

Puppies need to be fed a highly nutritious, good quality diet for them to develop and grow as they should. As a rough guide, a Jagdterrier puppy can be fed the following amounts every day making sure their meals are evenly spread out throughout the day and it's best to feed

Jagdterrier Dog Breed

them 3 or 4 times a day:

2 months old - 56 g to 152 g depending on a puppy's build

3 months old - 65 g to 179 g depending on a puppy's build

4 months old - 68 g to 190 g depending on a puppy's build

5 months old - 68 g to 193 g depending on a puppy's build

6 months old - 61 g to 193 g depending on a puppy's build

7 months old - 54 g to 174 g depending on a puppy's build

8 months old - 46 g to 156 g depending on a puppy's build

9 months old - 46 g to 139 g depending on a puppy's build

10 months old - 45 g to 138 g depending on a puppy's build

Once a puppy is 12 months old they can be fed adult dog food.

Feeding guide for an adult Jagdterrier

Once fully mature, an adult Jagdterrier must be fed a good quality diet to ensure their continued good health. As a rough guide, an adult Jagdterrier can be fed the following amounts every day:

Dogs weighing 7.5 kg can be fed 94g to 154g depending on activity

Dogs weighing 8.5 kg can be fed 114g to 174g depending on activity

Dogs weighing 9 kg can be fed 124 g to 184 g depending on a dog's build

Dogs weighing 10 kg can be fed 135 g to 206 g depending on a dog's build

Jagdterrier Dog Breed

Average Cost to Keep for Jagdterrier

Jagdterrier Dog Breed

If you are looking to buy a Jagdterrier, you would need to register your interest with breeders and agree to being put on a waiting list because very few puppies are bred and registered with The Kennel Club every year. You would need to pay anything upwards of £500 for a well-bred puppy.

The cost of insuring a male 3-year-old Jagdterrier in northern England would be £21.45 a month for basic cover but for a lifetime policy, this would set you back £43.22 a month (quote as of January 2018). When insurance companies calculate a pet's premium, they factor in several things which includes where you live in the UK, a dog's age and whether they have been neutered or spayed among other things.

When it comes to food costs, you need to buy the best quality food whether wet or dry making sure it suits the different stages of a dog's life. This would set you back between £20 - £30 a month. On top of this, you need to factor in veterinary costs if you want to share your home with a Jagdterrier and this includes their initial vaccinations, their annual boosters, the cost of neutering or spaying a dog when the time is right and their yearly health checks, all of which quickly adds up to over £800 a year.

As a rough guide, the average cost to keep and care for a Jagdterrier would be between £50 to £80 a month depending on the level of insurance cover you opt to buy for your dog, but this does not include the initial cost of buying a healthy, well-bred Jagdterrier puppy that's been bred from health tested parent dogs.

How to Identify A Jagdterrier

Method 1: Considering the Body Structure

1, Look at the dog's size. Jagdterriers are usually anywhere from 13–16 inches (33–41 cm) tall, and they typically weigh somewhere between 17–22 pounds (7.7–10.0 kg).

Jagdterrier Dog Breed

2, Examine the dog's head overall. Jagdterriers should have an elongated head overall that is shaped a little like a wedge (it should not be pointed), with a muzzle that should be a little shorter than their skull.

3, See what the dog's ears look like. Jagdterriers should have high-set ears that are in the shape of a V and not clearly small. Their ears should be in a semi-drop manner and touch a little.

4, View the dog's eyes. Jagdterriers should have dark-colored, oval-shaped eyes that are of a small size and set deep.

5, Check the dog's tail. About 1/3 of a Jagdterrier's tail is typically docked. It should be set well to their croup, and tends more often to be carried raised a little. The tail may also be natural, in which case it is in a manner that is horizontal or a little like a saber.

Jagdterrier Dog Breed

6, Take note of the dog's overall appearance. Overall, Jagdterriers should appear to be proportioned well and compact, with a free gait that covers a good amount of ground.

Method 2: Looking at the Coat

1, See what color the dog's coat is. Jagdterriers may be either dark brown, greyish-black, or black in color, and they should also have markings of a yellow-red color that are defined clearly and found on the dog's chest, muzzle, tail base, legs, and eyebrows. Sometimes, white-colored markings that are small in size may also be noticed on their toes and chest. You may also notice that the dog has a mask that is either dark or light in color.

2, Feel the coat's texture. Jagdterriers should have a coat that is either smooth and coarse or rough and hard in texture.

3, View the coat's overall appearance. Overall, Jagdterriers should have a coat with a plain appearance that is also dense.

Method 3: Examining Temperament

1, Find out if the dog is trainable. Jagdterriers are smart dogs, and therefore, quite trainable. However, because of the fact that the dog is smart, they will need a lot of mental stimulation, so be sure to keep that in mind.

Jagdterrier Dog Breed

2, Take note of courage. Jagdterriers are courageous and tenacious dogs overall who, when provoked, are not afraid to take on another dog, no matter how big they are compared to the Jagdterrier. Therefore, this dog will need proper socialization from an early age so they learn how to better interact with other dogs. They also are known to protect their family whenever they think something is a threat to them.

3, Look for a lot of energy. Jagdterriers are energetic dogs that generally need plenty of exercise every day, through things like walks or games of fetch.

4, Be aware of a high prey drive. Jagdterriers are known to have a high prey drive, meaning they generally will most likely not do well with cats or other small animals as they may chase them.

5, Understand that this dog needs a job of some sort. Jagdterriers generally do best if they have a job of some sort. If this job is not hunting, canine sports such as agility or frisbee can be some other great "jobs" for a Jagdterrier to do.